LUSCIOUS AFTERNOON TEAS

A Taste of Indulgence

LUSCIOUS AFTERNOON TEAS

ROSEMARY WADEY

CASSELL

First published in the UK in 1995 by
Cassell
Wellington House
125 Strand
London WC2R OBB

by arrangement with Lansdowne Publishing Pty Ltd
Level 5, 70 George Street, Sydney 2000, Australia

Managing Director: Jane Curry
Publishing Manager: Deborah Nixon
Production Manager: Sally Stokes
Project Co-ordinator: Pamela Brewster
Copy Editor: Lisa Foulis
Design: Modern Times Pty Ltd
Photographer: André Martin
Stylist: Donna Hay
Typeset in Garamond on Pagemaker
Printed in Singapore by Kyodo Printing Co. Pte

British Library Cataloguing-in-Publication Data
A catalogue record for this book is available from the British Library

ISBN 0-304-34756-6

Front cover: Chocolate Fudge Cake, recipe page 27
Page 2: Belgian Torte, recipe page 15
Back cover: Brandy Snaps, recipe page 19

Contents

Introduction

It is said that the British invented the meal called "afternoon tea". This meal does not actually exist in any other country, except where the British have had some influence in the community.

It used to be an elegant meal served mid-afternoon from a silver tray set beautifully with a lace cloth, silver teapot and the finest bone china cups. There would be wafer-thin sandwiches with fillings such as cucumber, or egg and cress; thinly sliced brown bread and butter, toast, muffins or crumpets; or warmed scones to serve with butter and homemade preserves often accompanied by a spoonful of thickly whipped or more likely clotted cream. The meal would be completed with a traditional cake such as a madeira, seed cake or light fruit cake along with delicious buttery shortbread fingers and all washed down with a cup, or indeed several cups, of tea.

Tea itself comes mainly from China, India and Ceylon and when first introduced was always drunk without the addition of milk. In the mid-seventeenth century the idea of mixing milk was introduced — initially in China, strangely enough, although it didn't last for long there — however the idea did spread worldwide and now tea is drunk either with milk or without depending on the type of tea and personal taste.

There are many types of tea available today, these having resulted from blending and mixing over the years. Popular Indian teas include Assam, Darjeeling and Mysore to name a few; while the best-loved China teas include Lapsong Souchong, Keemin and Earl Grey. Nowadays there are a great many fruit- and herb-flavoured teas on the market which have a great following.

Appetites must have been pretty large in olden days for the afternoon tea meal was "sandwiched" (for want of a better description) between a good three-course lunch and a four- or five-course dinner.

It was also a very important time for ladies to entertain their friends and acquaintances with an invitation to "take afternoon tea", often widely sought in society particularly by those wanting to climb the social ladder. Young ladies were taken to tea and shown off to prospective families, where their suitability as a potential wife for the young gentleman of the family was assessed.

In winter time this ritual afternoon tea was taken around a blazing log fire in the drawing room, while in summer the tables were laid out on lawns beneath the shade of the trees. The ladies hosting these parties sought to outdo each other with the selection of delicacies offered, and here began the ritual of luscious afternoon teas, offered and enjoyed as a taste of indulgence. The sandwiches became thinner and more elegant, the scones were mouth-watering morsels and the cakes and pastries became masterpieces in their own rights. There would be airy choux concoctions, pastry so light it could hardly cause any problems to the waistline and numerous cakes and gateaux of every conceivable shape, size, taste and texture filled and topped with cream, crème au beurre, pastry cream and all types of fruits subtly glazed and then encased in yet more cream. Chocolate, coffee, citrus were very popular as were other ingredients including a variety of nuts, fresh and dried fruits and many more.

The lower and middle classes didn't keep to the ritual of afternoon tea but preferred a high tea, a type of tea and supper combined to serve very early in the evening. This meal, too, would always contain one or two cakes or pastries to accompany whatever else was served. These cakes were often served as an indulgence from the normal fare, particularly on a Sunday when all the family would be assembled.

When it comes to other indulgent teas the Tea Dance was very popular. Cups of tea were served in preference to alcoholic drinks along with a selection of delectable tea-time fare; ladies gathered in large numbers to dance the afternoon away with an array of young men, at the same time indulging themselves in luscious tea-time fare.

Tennis teas were also popular from the early 1900s for young and old alike. After the exertions of a game of tennis a tea was laid out in a shady area of the garden, the array being a delight to the eye and fit to tempt both players and onlookers. However, in this case it was usually served as a buffet with members of the family or servants in attendance and iced tea and cold drinks were offered along with the traditional pot of tea.

When it comes to choosing the selection of cakes, gateaux and pastries for inclusion in a title such as *Luscious Afternoon Teas*, the list is unending. For a start there are the small cakes and pastries, all baked individually with each one requiring its own specific preparation and decorations; meringues, tuile mixtures, puff and filo pastry, choux paste, yeasted pastries and many more with tastes to suit everyone and cream in abundance. Individual pastries come in all sizes and with a base of paté sucrée, paté brisée and short crust; the fillings of fresh and poached fruits are mixed with or laid over things such as syllabub, whipped cream or pastry cream with a glaze added to the fruits for that special finish.

Cakes that are baked in trays are easy to make and look attractive both whole or cut into fingers or squares. It is the way the topping, strips of pastry or decoration of cream is added that gives it a touch of luxury both in appearance and taste.

The list of large cakes and gateaux is almost interminable and it is with difficulty that the selection of recipes for this book was finally chosen. Indulgence to my mind means forget the calories and cholesterol, look for the creamiest, most mouth-watering concoction you can find and then really indulge yourself with a big slice — and if the feeling takes you, have another slice! It is not always possible to indulge in true luxury and luscious fare, but life is too short to diet forever and when the opportunity is there to participate in a luscious tea, whether you are the cook or the guest or both, then let yourself go and be really and truly indulgent. After all, you can always count the calories tomorrow!

THE RECIPES

Almond Cornets

2 egg whites
4 oz (125 g) superfine (caster) sugar
2 oz (60 g) all-purpose (plain) flour,
    sifted twice
2 oz (60 g) flaked almonds, finely
    chopped
2 oz (60 g) butter, melted and cooled

few drops almond extract (essence)
finely grated peel (rind)) of 1 orange
FILLING:
1 cup (8 fl oz/250 ml) heavy (double)
    cream
1 tablespoon curacao or Grand Marnier

LINE two or three baking sheets with non-stick parchment (baking paper). Grease three or four cream horn shapes. Whisk the egg whites in a clean grease-free bowl until very stiff and dry and standing in peaks. Fold in the sugar, then the flour and almonds, evenly but lightly. Fold in the butter, extract and orange peel.

Place heaped teaspoons of the mixture well apart on the baking sheets and spread out thinly — three or four per sheet is ample. Cook in a moderately hot oven (375°F/190°C/Gas Mark 5) for 8–12 minutes or until just tinged brown around the edges and golden brown in the middle.

Cool very slightly on the baking sheets then remove quickly and wind around the cream horn shapes so the tip is tight and closed. Leave until firm, then carefully ease off cornet shapes and place on a wire rack until cold. Lightly re-grease the cream horn shapes.

Bake another batch and shape in the same way. At this stage the cornets may be stored in an airtight container for several days before filling.

Whip the cream with the liqueur until stiff. Put into a piping bag fitted with a large star vegetable nozzle and carefully pipe the cream into the cornets, finishing with an attractive twist. Serve within about an hour of filling or they may begin to soften.

Makes about 16

> •
> Use grated lemon or lime peel (rind) in place of the orange peel and replace the nuts with finely chopped toasted hazelnuts or pecan nuts for a change.
> •

Almond Fingers

4 oz (125 g) unblanched almonds

3 oz (90 g) all-purpose (plain) flour

2 oz (60 g) self-rising (raising) flour

3 oz (90 g) all-purpose (plain) wholewheat flour

4 level tablespoons light soft brown sugar

4 oz (125 g) butter or margarine

grated peel (rind) of 1 orange

2 eggs, separated

1–2 tablespoons milk

4 oz (125 g) coarse orange marmalade, apricot jam or ginger preserve

12 oz (375 g) confectioners' (icing) sugar, sifted

PLACE the almonds in a bowl, cover with boiling water and leave for about 5 minutes. Drain and peel off the skins, and while still moist cut into slivers (about four per almond). Alternately use flaked almonds.

Line a rectangular pan of approximately 11 x 7 x 1½ inches (28 x 18 x 4 cm) with non-stick parchment (baking paper).

Sift the white flours together and mix in the wholewheat flour and sugar, then rub in the butter until the mixture resembles fine breadcrumbs. Add the orange peel, egg yolks and sufficient milk to bind to a pliable dough that is slightly on the soft side.

Press the dough into the lined pan, keeping it as even as possible. Spread the marmalade, jam or preserve evenly over it.

Whisk the egg whites until really frothy — halfway to meringue — then beat in the confectioners' sugar. Spread evenly over the dough and sprinkle with the slivered almonds.

Cook in a very moderate oven (325°F/170°C/Gas Mark 3) for 40–50 minutes, until lightly browned.

Leave in the pan to cool slightly, then cut carefully into fingers or squares while still warm. When cold, remove from the pan.

Makes about 14

Belgian Torte

8 oz (250 g) butter
3 oz (90 g) superfine (caster) sugar
2 tablespoons oil
½ teaspoon vanilla extract (essence)
few drops almond extract (essence)
1 egg, beaten
1 lb (500 g) all-purpose (plain) flour
1 level teaspoon double-acting baking
    powder (2 level teaspoons baking
    powder)

12 oz (375 g) apricot jam or preserve
5–6 oz (150–175 g) dried apricots,
    chopped
2 tablespoons brandy
grated peel (rind) of 1 small orange
a little confectioners' (icing) sugar to
    decorate

> •
> *This torte can be frozen for two to three months. It may also be decorated around the top edge with well-drained apricot halves that have been brushed with sieved apricot jam.*
> •

GREASE a 8 inch (20 cm) round spring form cake pan and line the base of the cake pan with non-stick parchment (baking paper).

Cream the butter and the sugar until light in tone and fluffy. Beat in the oil, the extracts and the egg. Sift the flour and baking powder together and gradually work in to the creamed mixture. Knead together as if making a shortbread dough, until smooth. Divide the dough into three portions and coarsely grate one portion into the cake pan so it covers the base evenly.

Combine the jam, apricots, brandy and orange peel and spread half of it over the grated dough; grate the second portion of the dough over the apricots. Spread the rest of the apricot mixture over the grated dough. Grate the remaining dough over the top.

Cook in a cool oven (300°F/150°C/Gas Mark 2) for about 1½ hours until lightly browned. Remove from the oven and leave until cool, loosening the torte from the sides of the pan with a palette knife as it cools.

When cold remove from the pan and either wrap in foil and keep for two to three days or, if serving at once, dredge with confectioners' sugar and cut into wedges.

Blueberry Cheese Boats

PATE SUCREE:

6 oz (175 g) all-purpose (plain) flour

pinch of salt

3 oz (90 g) superfine (caster) sugar

3 oz (90 g) butter, slightly softened

3 egg yolks

TOPPING:

8 oz (250 g) blackcurrants or blueberries,
    fresh or thawed if frozen

FILLING:

8 oz (250 g) full fat soft cream cheese

3 tablespoons clear honey

grated peel (rind) of ½ orange or lemon
    or of 1 lime

large pinch of ground cinnamon or
    ground allspice

5 fl oz (150 ml) heavy (double) cream

TO MAKE the pastry, sift the flour and salt onto a flat surface and make a well in the middle. Add the sugar, butter and egg yolks to the well. Gradually work in the flour to give a smooth pliable dough. Wrap in plastic (cling) wrap and chill for 1 hour.

Roll out the pastry and use to line 10 to 12 boat moulds. Bake blind for about 10 minutes in a moderately hot oven (375°F/190°C/Gas Mark 5). Cool on a wire rack.

To make the filling, beat the cheese until smooth then beat in the honey, fruit peel and spice. Whip the cream until stiff and fold about a third of it into the cheese mixture. Divide the cheesecake mixture between the pastry boats levelling the tops.

Decorate the boats with the fruit. Using the remaining whipped cream pipe a whirl in the middle of each boat.

Makes 10–12

Brandy Snaps

2 oz (60 g) butter or margarine
2 oz (60 g) superfine (caster) sugar
2 oz (60 g) light treacle (golden syrup)
2 oz (60 g) all-purpose (plain) flour
¼ level teaspoon ground ginger

FILLING:
1 cup (8 fl oz/250 ml) heavy (double)
   cream
few pieces stem or crystallized ginger,
   finely chopped

IT IS essential to bake these biscuits in batches, and if possible put the mixture onto cold baking sheets for the best results.

Line three or four baking sheets with non-stick parchment (baking paper). Grease two or three wooden spoon handles and/or four to six cream horn shapes.

Melt the butter in a saucepan with the sugar and treacle over a gentle heat; remove from the heat. Sift the flour and ginger together and beat into the melted mixture. Put four teaspoons of the mixture onto the lined baking sheets, keeping them well apart. (For mini brandy snaps to use as petit fours, use small spoonfuls of the mixture.)

Cook in a very moderate oven (325°F/170°C/Gas Mark 3) for about 10 minutes or until an even golden brown. Allow to cool briefly, pushing the edges back into shape with a small round-bladed knife, then carefully ease off the paper, one at a time, and immediately wind round a greased wooden spoon handle or cream horn shape. Quickly shape the others before they set. If the mixture becomes too firm, replace in the oven for a minute or so and then try again.

Cool on a wire rack until firm, then slide off the handles or tins. Cook and shape the remaining mixture in the same way. Store in an airtight container for up to 2 weeks, until required.

To serve, whip the cream until stiff and if liked add a few pieces of ginger, then fill the snaps or cones using a piping bag fitted with a large star piping nozzle.

Makes 12–16

•

For brandy baskets, grease the base and sides of several small cups or ramekin dishes and as the brandy biscuits are ready, lay over the base and shape to the sides of the container. The biscuits should be made a little larger e.g. 2 teaspoons of the mixture, and if they are too big for the ramekins, simply spread out over the surface to give a "lip". As soon as they are firm, remove and cool the right way up on a wire rack.

•

Cherry Dessert Cake

4 oz (125 g) butter or margarine
5½ oz (165 g) self-rising (raising) flour
½ level teaspoon double-acting baking
    powder (1 level teaspoon baking
    powder)
2 eggs, beaten
4 oz (125 g) superfine (caster) sugar
1½ tablespoons white wine
1½ teaspoons rose water
    (triple strength)
½ level teaspoon grated or ground
    nutmeg
8 oz (250 g) fresh cherries, pitted or a
    15 oz (450 g) can black cherries,
    thoroughly drained and pitted
superfine (caster) sugar for dredging
6 tablespoons heavy (double) cream
4 tablespoons thick natural yogurt

GREASE and line an 7–8 inch (18–20 cm) round spring form cake pan with non-stick parchment (baking paper).

Melt the butter in a saucepan and then cool until only barely warm but not set. Sift in the flour and baking powder and mix into the butter with the eggs, sugar, wine, rose water and nutmeg; beat well by hand or with an electric whisk.

Pour half the mixture into the prepared pan, arrange the cherries over it and then add the remaining mixture, making sure all the cherries are covered.

Cook in a moderate oven (350°F/180°C/Gas Mark 4) for about 45 minutes or until golden brown and a skewer inserted in the middle comes out clean.

Cool in the pan for a few minutes then remove carefully onto a wire rack. Dredge with superfine sugar and leave until cold.

If desired, whip the cream until stiff and carefully fold in the yogurt. Put into a piping bag fitted with a large star nozzle and pipe a decoration on top of the cake.

Chocolate and Hazelnut Caramels

BASE:

6 oz (175 g) all-purpose (plain) flour

pinch of salt

2 oz (60 g) light soft brown sugar or
  superfine (caster) sugar

4 oz (125 g) butter

1½ oz (40 g) toasted hazelnuts, chopped

grated peel (rind) of 1 orange

FILLING:

4 oz (125 g) margarine

4 oz (125 g) light soft brown sugar

2 tablespoons light treacle (golden syrup)

1 small or ½ large can condensed milk

few drops almond extract (essence)

TOPPING:

3 oz (90 g) semi-sweet (plain) chocolate

½ oz (15 g) butter

2 oz (60 g) white chocolate

To MAKE the base, grease a 7 inch (18 cm) square shallow cake pan. Sift the flour and salt. Add the sugar and rub in the butter then mix in the chopped nuts and grated peel. Work into a pliable dough and press evenly into the prepared pan. Cook in a moderate oven (350°F/180°C/Gas Mark 4) for about 25 minutes or until pale golden brown and just firm. Cool in the pan.

To make the filling, put the margarine, sugar, treacle and condensed milk into a saucepan and gently bring to a boil. Boil gently for 7–8 minutes, stirring occasionally and taking care it does not "catch". Add almond extract and beat until beginning to thicken. Pour over the base, cool and then chill thoroughly until set.

To make the topping, melt the chocolate with the butter over a pan of simmering water; stir until evenly blended. Melt the white chocolate separately.

Spread the semi-sweet chocolate over the caramel, making sure it fills the corners. Let it set slightly then drizzle the white chocolate over it. Leave until completely set, then cut into fingers or squares.

Makes 14–16

Chocolate Battenberg

4 oz (125 g) superfine (caster) sugar
4 oz (125 g) butter or soft margarine
2 eggs
4 oz (125 g) self-rising (raising) flour,
   sifted
1 tablespoon cold water
1 teaspoon coffee extract (essence)

2 level teaspoons cocoa powder
TOPPING:
8 oz (250 g) white marzipan
few chocolate coffee beans or chocolate
   matchsticks
Chocolate butter cream

GREASE and line a 8 inch (20 cm) square cake pan with non-stick parchment (baking paper), making a pleat down the middle which stands up about 1 ½ inches (4 cm). This divides the pan so that the two cakes can be baked at the same time.

Cream the sugar and butter together until very light and fluffy then beat in the eggs one at a time, following each with a spoonful of the flour. Beat in the rest of the flour with the water. Divide the mixture in half and add the coffee extract to one part and the cocoa to the other. Spread the mixtures in the two sections in the pan. Cook in a moderate oven (350°F/180°C/Gas Mark 4) for about 30 minutes or until well risen and firm to the touch. Turn out onto a wire rack and leave until cold.

Remove the paper from the cakes and stand one on top of the other. Trim so they are equal in size, then cut in half lengthwise and reverse the cakes so the chocolate and coffee pieces are reversed to give a checkerboard. Spread some of the butter cream over the pieces so they stick together and then spread a little more around the sides of the cake.

Roll out the marzipan to a rectangle just large enough to enclose the cake, stand the cake on it and wrap around to fit, keeping the joins underneath. Trim the ends so the cake is even, then mark a light crisscross design along the top of the cake.

Put the remaining butter cream into a piping bag fitted with a star nozzle and pipe a decoration along the top of the cake. Decorate with chocolate beans or sticks.

CHOCOLATE BUTTER CREAM

•

3 oz (90 g) butter,
preferably unsalted
6 oz (175 g) confectioners'
(icing) sugar, sifted
1 ½ level tablespoons cocoa
powder, sifted
2–3 teaspoons milk
few drops vanilla extract
(essence)

•

To make the filling, cream the butter with the sugar and cocoa and add sufficient milk to give a spreading consistency; add a few drops of vanilla.

•

Chocolate Fudge Cake

3 oz (90 g) butter or soft margarine

4 oz (125 g) superfine (caster) sugar

5 oz (150 g) light soft brown sugar

10 oz (300 g) all-purpose (plain) flour

2 level teaspoons baking soda
(bicarbonate of soda)

2 level tablespoons cocoa powder

4 eggs

4 oz (125 g) semi-sweet (plain) chocolate,
melted

1 level tablespoon dark treacle

1 teaspoon vanilla extract (essence)

7 fl oz (200 ml) milk

Chocolate fudge frosting

GREASE and line the base of three 8½–9 inch (21–23 cm) deep sandwich pans with greased waxed (greaseproof) paper or non-stick parchment (baking paper) and dust lightly with flour.

Cream the butter and sugars until light and fluffy. Sift the flour, baking soda and cocoa powder together. Beat the eggs into the creamed mixture one at a time, following each with a spoonful of the flour mixture. Beat in the chocolate, treacle and extract and then fold in the remainder of the flour alternately with the milk until smooth. Divide between the pans, level the tops and cook in a moderate oven (350°F/180°C/Gas Mark 4) for about 30–40 minutes or until well risen and firm to the touch. Loosen from the pans and turn out carefully onto wire racks. Strip off the paper and leave until cold.

Use some of the frosting to sandwich the cakes together; stand on a plate. Use the remaining frosting to cover the top of the cake and then swirl it attractively before it begins to set. Leave to set before serving. If desired the cake may be very lightly dredged with confectioners' sugar.

NOTE: The un-iced cakes may be frozen for up to three months. Add the frosting when completely thawed.

CHOCOLATE FUDGE

FROSTING

•

7 oz (200 g) semi-sweet
(plain) chocolate

1½ oz (40 g) blended
white fat

few drops vanilla extract
(essence)

8 oz (250 g)
confectioners' (icing)
sugar, sifted

4 tablespoons milk

•

Break up the chocolate into a heatproof bowl and add the fat and extract. Stand over a pan of gently simmering water until completely melted. Add the confectioners' sugar and milk and beat until evenly mixed. Remove from the heat and beat until quite smooth.

•

Chocolate Meringues

3 egg whites
6 oz (175 g) superfine (caster)
    sugar
2 oz (60 g) semi-sweet (plain)
    chocolate, grated
DECORATION:
⅔ cup (10 fl oz/300 ml) heavy
    (double) cream
1 tablespoon rum

1½ oz (40 g) pistachio nuts, blanched
    and chopped
or 1½ oz (40 g) toasted hazelnuts,
    finely chopped
or 1 oz (30 g) unsweetened (desiccated)
    or shredded coconut, lightly toasted
or 1 oz (30 g) semi-sweet (plain)
    chocolate, grated

LINE two baking sheets with non-stick parchment (baking paper).

Put the egg whites into a clean grease-free bowl and whisk until very stiff and dry and standing in peaks. Whisk in the sugar about 1 tablespoon at a time, making sure the mixture is stiff again before adding further sugar. When all the sugar is incorporated and the meringue is very stiff, fold in the grated chocolate evenly. Put into a piping bag fitted with a ¾ inch (2 cm) plain vegetable nozzle. Pipe the meringue into fingers approx. 3 inches (7.5 cm) long (making 20–24) onto the parchment (baking paper).

Cook in a cool oven (225°F/110°C/Gas Mark ¼) for about 1½–1¾ hours or until firm and dry and the meringues easily peel off the paper. Leave to cool.

Whip the cream with the rum until just stiff. Put into a piping bag fitted with a large star vegetable nozzle and pipe a line on one meringue finger and cover with another. Sprinkle liberally with chopped nuts, coconut or chocolate and arrange on a serving plate.

Makes 10–12 pairs

> The mixture may also be piped into stars, shells or whirls if preferred, using a large star vegetable nozzle. They may be part dipped in chocolate or a layer of chocolate spread over the flat surface. Sandwich together in pairs with whipped cream.

Chocolate Roulade

5 eggs, separated
6 oz (175 g) superfine (caster) sugar
6 oz (175 g) semi-sweet (plain dark)
    chocolate
2 tablespoons hot water
FILLING:
1¼ cups (10 fl oz/300 ml) heavy
    (double) cream

2 tablespoons orange liqueur
grated peel (rind) of 1 small
    orange (optional) or a 9 oz (275 g)
    can sweetened chestnut spread
confectioners' (icing) sugar, for
    decoration
8 Chocolate leaves

LINE a 13 x 9 inch (33 x 25 cm) jelly (Swiss) roll pan with non-stick parchment (baking paper). Whisk the egg yolks and sugar together until pale and fluffy either over a pan of gently simmering water or in an electric mixer. Melt the chocolate over a pan of simmering water. Stir through the whisked mixture followed by the water. Whisk the egg whites until stiff and dry and fold into the chocolate mixture. Pour into the prepared pan, spreading it evenly.

Cook in a moderately hot oven (375°F/190°C/Gas Mark 5) for 15–20 minutes or until the surface is crusty, puffy and just firm. Cover with a sheet of non-stick parchment (baking paper) and a damp cloth and leave until completely cold, preferably overnight.

Turn out onto a large piece of waxed (greaseproof) paper dusted with confectioners' sugar. Remove the lining paper and trim the edges of the cake.

Whip the cream with the liqueur until stiff and put about one third into a piping bag fitted with a large star nozzle. Add the orange peel to the remaining cream, if used, or beat in the chestnut spread until smooth. Spread the cream mixture all over the cake. Using the paper to help, carefully roll up to enclose the cream and transfer to a serving plate. Dredge with sifted sugar. Pipe a cream decoration along the top of the roulade and add the chocolate leaves. Chill until required.

CHOCOLATE LEAVES

•

Select unblemished rose leaves, wash and dry thoroughly. Using melted chocolate and a paint brush, carefully coat the underside of each leaf evenly with chocolate, taking care not to get any chocolate on the tops of the leaves. When set add a second coat. Place on non-stick parchment (baking paper), chocolate facing upwards, and put in the refrigerator or in a cool place until set hard. When required, carefully peel the rose leaves away from the chocolate.

•

Cigarellos

2 egg whites
4 oz (125 g) superfine (caster) sugar
1½ oz (40 g) all-purpose (plain)
    flour, sifted
1¾ oz (45 g) butter, melted and
    cooled

few drops almond extract (essence)
(optional)
TO DECORATE:
2 oz (60 g) semi-sweet (plain) chocolate,
    melted
1½ oz (40 g) pistachio nuts, blanched
    and finely chopped

LINE two baking sheets with non-stick parchment (baking paper). Grease two or three thick straight skewers or narrow pencils.

Whisk the egg whites in a clean grease-free bowl until very stiff and dry and standing in peaks. Gradually fold in the sugar, then the flour and finally the melted butter and extract until evenly but lightly mixed.

Spread the mixture fairly thinly into oblongs about 4 x 3 inches (10 x 7.5 cm), placing only two or three per baking sheet.

Cook in a fairly hot oven (400°F/200°C/Gas Mark 6) for about 8 minutes or until lightly browned.

Remove the biscuits one at a time, using a round-bladed palette knife and place upside down on another piece of parchment (baking paper). Quickly roll around the skewers or pencils. Slide off quickly and cool on a wire rack. If the biscuits become too firm to roll, return briefly to the oven to soften again.

To decorate, melt the chocolate and dip one or both ends of the cigarellos in the chocolate so they are evenly coated and then sprinkle with chopped pistachio nuts. Leave to set.

Makes about 16

Coconut Frosted Marbled Ring

8 oz (250 g) self-rising (raising) flour
¾ level teaspoon double-acting baking
    powder (1½ level teaspoons baking
    powder)
6 oz (175 g) superfine (caster) sugar
6 oz (175 g) soft tub margarine
3 eggs
5 tablespoons orange juice

grated peel (rind) of 2 oranges
few drops orange food dye
½ teaspoon vanilla extract (essence)
2 tablespoons Cointreau
TO DECORATE:
Seven minute frosting
2 oz (60 g) shredded coconut or coconut
    strands, lightly toasted

GREASE a 5 cup (2 pint/1.1 litre) ring pan and dust the inside lightly with flour.

Sift the flour and baking powder into a bowl, add the sugar, margarine, eggs and 3 tablespoons orange juice and beat well for 2 minutes, preferably with an electric mixer, until smooth and evenly blended. Remove half the mixture to another bowl.

Add the orange peel and orange food dye to the original bowl of mixture until pale orange. Add the vanilla to the other bowl.

Put alternate tablespoons of the mixtures into the ring pan and if liked run a sharp knife around the pan to stir it even more. Level the top.

Cook in a very moderate oven (325°F/170°C/Gas Mark 3) for about 45 minutes or until well risen and firm to the touch.

Cool for a few minutes in the pan, until it begins to come away from the sides, then turn out carefully onto a wire rack and leave until cold. Combine remaining orange juice and Cointreau and spoon over the top of the cake.

Spread and swirl Seven minute frosting all over the cake and sprinkle quickly with the toasted coconut before it has time to set.

SEVEN MINUTE FROSTING

•

1 egg white
5 oz (150 g) superfine
(caster) sugar
pinch of salt
2 tablespoons water
pinch of cream of tartar

•

Put all the ingredients into a heatproof bowl and mix lightly. Stand over a saucepan of gently simmering water and beat well, preferably with a hand-held electric mixer until thick enough to stand in peaks. Remove from the heat and use at once.

•

Coffee Puffs

2½ oz (65 g) all-purpose (plain) flour
pinch of salt
2 oz (60 g) butter
⅔ cup (5 fl oz/150 ml) water
2 eggs, beaten
Praline cream

COFFEE GLACE ICING:
6 oz (175 g) confectioners' (icing) sugar, sifted
2–3 teaspoons coffee extract (essence) or very strong black coffee

TO MAKE the choux puffs, sift the flour and salt together. Put the butter and water into a saucepan and gently bring to a boil. Add the flour all at once and mix with a wooden spoon until the paste forms a ball and leaves the sides of the pan clean.

Remove from the heat and spread the paste out evenly over the base of the pan. Leave to cool for about 10 minutes, then beat the eggs vigorously into the paste, a little at a time, until smooth and glossy; a hand-held electric mixer is best for this job. The paste may not need all of the egg. Put the paste into a piping bag fitted with a ¾ inch (2 cm) plain vegetable nozzle and pipe round balls about one and a half times the size of a walnut, well apart, onto well-greased baking sheets. Cook in a hot oven (425°F/220°C/Gas Mark 7) for 25–30 minutes or until well puffed up, golden brown and firm to the touch. Remove from the oven and pierce each one close to the base with a skewer to allow the steam to escape. Return to the turned-off oven for 2–3 minutes to dry out. Cool on a wire rack.

Put the Praline cream into a piping bag fitted with a ¼ inch (5 mm) plain piping nozzle, carefully insert the nozzle in the holes in the bases of the choux puffs, and pipe in the cream filling.

Place the confectioners' sugar in a bowl and gradually work in the coffee extract (plus a little hot water if necessary) to give a thick consistency. Carefully dip the top of each bun in the icing so it is well covered, then leave to set on a wire rack.

Makes 14–16

PRALINE CREAM

•

3 oz (90 g) unblanched almonds

3 oz (90 g) superfine (caster) sugar

1¼ cups (10 fl oz/300 ml) heavy (double) cream

•

Put the almonds and sugar into a heavy-based pan and heat gently until the sugar has melted. Cook slowly until golden brown, then turn quickly onto an oiled baking sheet or piece of non-stick parchment (baking paper). Leave until cold and set and then crush with a rolling pin. Whip the cream and fold in the praline.

•

Cream Meringues

2 egg whites
4 oz (125 g) superfine (caster) sugar
FILLING:
1 cup (8 fl oz/250 ml) heavy (double)
    cream

1 tablespoon liqueur, rum or brandy
    (optional)
2 oz (60 g) semi-sweet (plain) chocolate

LINE two or three baking sheets with non-stick parchment (baking paper).

Put the egg whites in a clean grease-free bowl and whisk until very stiff and dry and standing in peaks.

Whisk in the sugar a tablespoon at a time, making sure the meringue is stiff again before adding further sugar.

Place the meringue in a large piping bag fitted with a large star vegetable nozzle and pipe into 1½ inch (4 cm) wide shells, rosettes, whirls or stars. Alternately use a ½–¾ inch (1½–2 cm) plain vegetable nozzle and pipe similar shapes onto the baking sheets, or simply spoon the meringue into even heaps using two dessertspoons to help shape them.

Cook in a very cool oven (225°F/110°C/Gas Mark ¼) for 1½–2 hours or until crisp and dry and they peel easily off the paper. Leave to cool on the baking sheets. Unfilled meringues will store in an airtight container for up to two weeks.

To serve, whip the cream with the liqueur, if used, until stiff and then put into a piping bag fitted with a large star vegetable nozzle and pipe a whirl onto the base of one meringue and sandwich together with another one. Melt the chocolate in a bowl over a pan of gently simmering water, stir until smooth then drizzle chocolate over the meringues.

Makes about 12 pairs

BROWN SUGAR
MERINGUES

•

Replace half the superfine sugar with light soft brown sugar and sift them together twice before you begin. The insides will be more gooey than normal meringues and sometimes may tend to stick to the paper a little more.

•

Danish Pastries

1 level teaspoon superfine (caster) sugar
about ⅔ cup (5 fl oz/150 ml) warm
    water
3 level teaspoons dried yeast
1 lb (500 g) all-purpose (plain) flour
    (not strong flour)
½ level teaspoon salt

2 oz (60 g) lard or white fat
1 oz (30 g) superfine (caster) sugar
2 eggs, beaten
10 oz (300 g) butter, softened
3 oz (90 g) marzipan
beaten egg to glaze

DISSOLVE the sugar in the water, sprinkle in the yeast and leave in a warm place for 10 minutes until frothy. Sift the flour and salt, rub in the fat, then mix in the sugar. Add the yeast liquid and eggs and mix to form a soft elastic dough, adding a little extra water if necessary. Knead lightly on a floured surface until smooth, about 3–4 minutes. Place in a lightly oiled polythene bag and chill for 10 minutes. Shape the butter into an oblong approximately 10 x 4 inches (25 x 10 cm).

Roll out the dough to a 11 inch (28 cm) square and spread the butter down the middle third. Enclose the butter by folding the two flaps of dough to just overlap in the middle; seal the top and bottom with a rolling pin. Roll out into a strip three times as long as it is wide, then fold the bottom third upwards and the top third down. Seal the edges. Return to the polythene bag and chill for 20 minutes.

Repeat this whole process twice more, then chill for at least 30 minutes. The dough is now ready for use. At this stage it may be frozen for up to three months.

WINDMILLS OR IMPERIAL STARS – Roll out a quarter of the dough and cut into 3 inch (7.5 cm) squares. Make diagonal cuts from each corner to within ½ inch (1 cm) of the middle. Put a small piece of marzipan in the middle. Fold one corner of each cut section to the middle of the square and seal with beaten egg. Put onto a greased baking sheet; put to rise in a warm place for 20–30 minutes or until puffy. Glaze with beaten egg and cook in a hot oven (425°F/220°C/Gas Mark 7) for about 20 minutes.

Makes about 28

COCK'S COMBS

•

Roll out a quarter of the dough thinly and cut into strips 4½ x 5 inches (11 x 12 cm). Spread half the width of each strip with a little marzipan, crème patissière (see page 51) or stewed apple sprinkled with cinnamon and currants. Fold over the other half to enclose the filling and seal with beaten egg. Make four or five cuts into the folded edge and place on greased baking sheets, curving a little to open out the comb. Put to rise, glaze and cook as for Windmills.

•

Dobos Torte

4 eggs
6 oz (175 g) superfine (caster) sugar
5 oz (150 g) all-purpose (plain) flour,
    sifted

TOPPING:
4 oz (125 g) superfine (caster) sugar
about 24 hazelnuts, toasted
Rich chocolate butter cream

DRAW FIVE rectangles 10 x 4½ inches (25 x 11 cm) on non-stick parchment (baking paper) and place on baking sheets.

Whisk the eggs and sugar together in a bowl over a pan of gently simmering water or in a large electric mixer until very pale and thick and the whisk leaves a heavy trail when lifted. Sift in the flour and fold in lightly and evenly.

Divide the mixture between the rectangles and spread out so they are completely covered. Cook in a moderately hot oven (375°F/190°C/Gas Mark 5) for about 10 minutes each or until golden brown and firm. Trim off the edges to fit the drawn shapes, peel carefully off the paper and leave on a wire rack until cold.

Select the best of the layers and keep aside. Put the superfine sugar into a heavy-based saucepan and heat gently until melted, then cook gently until the caramel turns a golden brown. Pour quickly over the selected layer so it is completely covered. As it dries, mark into even wedges using the back of a well-oiled knife.

Place a layer of cake on a serving dish and spread with butter cream. Layer up the rest of the torte using about a third of the butter cream. Put the caramel layer on top. Cover the sides of the torte with butter cream and decorate attractively using a fork, icing comb or palette knife. Decorate with hazelnuts.

RICH CHOCOLATE BUTTER CREAM

•

6 oz (175 g) butter, preferably unsalted

10 oz (300 g) confectioners' (icing) sugar, sifted

1 tablespoon rum or coffee liqueur

3 oz (90 g) semi-sweet (plain) chocolate, melted and cooled

•

Cream the butter until soft then gradually beat in the sugar, rum and chocolate until smooth.

•

Filo Mincemeat Bundles

6 oz (175 g) mincemeat
grated peel (rind) of 1 orange
2 tablespoon brandy or rum
2 dessert apples, peeled, cored and
    coarsely grated

2 level tablespoons chopped blanched
    almonds or hazelnuts
12 sheets filo pastry, thawed if frozen
about 3 oz (90 g) butter, melted
confectioners' (icing) sugar, for dredging

THESE bundles are a mixture of grated apple, orange peel, brandy and mincemeat encased in sheets of filo pastry pinched together at the top and dredged with confectioners' sugar.

Put the mincemeat into a bowl and mix in the orange peel and brandy. Add the apple and the nuts and mix well.

Cut each sheet of pastry in half to give two squares. Put one square on a flat surface and brush with melted butter. Place another square on top in a diamond position, about a 45° angle. Its corners should be midway between the corners of the first square. Brush again with melted butter.

Place a heaped teaspoon of the mincemeat mixture in the middle of the pastry and carefully gather up the edges and pinch tightly together, allowing the tips of the pastry to fall over. Stand on greased baking sheets and carefully brush all over with melted butter. Repeat with the rest of the pastry.

Cook in a moderately hot oven (375°F/190°C/Gas Mark 5) for about 20 minutes or until a light golden brown and the pastry is cooked through. Remove to a wire rack and dredge with sifted confectioners' sugar. Leave until cold, and serve as they are or with whipped cream.

Makes 12

Florentines

3 oz (90 g) butter
4 oz (125 g) superfine (caster) sugar
4 oz (125 g) flaked almonds
1 oz (30 g) seedless raisins, chopped
1½ oz (40 g) mixed peel, chopped
1½ oz (40 g) glacé cherries, chopped
finely grated peel (rind) of ½ lemon or
    orange

1 oz (30 g) crystallized pineapple or
    papaya, finely chopped
1 oz (30 g) stem or preserved ginger,
    chopped (optional)
about 6 oz (175 g) semi-sweet (plain)
    chocolate, melted

> •
> For a change, try using
> white chocolate for
> backing the Florentines.
> •

LINE three baking sheets with non-stick parchment (baking paper). Melt the butter and sugar in a saucepan and boil for 1 minute. Remove from the heat and stir in the remaining ingredients except the chocolate. Leave to cool.

Put teaspoonfuls of the mixture in heaps on the baking sheets, keeping well apart — a maximum of four per sheet for safety.

Cook in a moderate oven (350°F/180°C/Gas Mark 4) for 10–12 minutes or until golden brown. Using a small palette knife, push the cookies back into shape as they cool. Remove carefully to a wire rack using the knife and leave until quite cold and firm.

Melt the chocolate either in a microwave oven or in a heatproof bowl over a pan of gently simmering water. Spread over the back (the smooth side) of each Florentine and as it sets, mark into wavy lines using a fork. Leave to set.

The biscuits can be stored without the chocolate for up to a week between sheets of waxed or non-stick parchment (baking paper) in an airtight container. Spread with chocolate just before serving.

Makes 24–30

Fondant Fancies

3 eggs
3 oz (90 g) superfine (caster) sugar
2½ oz (75 g) all-purpose (plain) flour
1 level tablespoon cornstarch (cornflour)
pinch of double-acting baking powder
    (large pinch baking powder)
1½ oz (40 g) butter, melted and
    cooled

DECORATIONS:
8 level tablespoons apricot jam, sieved
3 oz (90 g) marzipan (yellow or white)
Fondant icing
edible food dyes
1 recipe quantity Glacé icing (page 69)

FONDANT ICING

•

1 lb (500 g) sugar
⅔ cup (5 fl oz/150 ml)
water
3 level tablespoons glucose
or a large pinch of cream
of tartar

•

In a heavy-based pan gently dissolve the sugar in the water. Bring to a boil, add the glucose or cream of tartar and boil without stirring, until it reaches the soft ball stage (240°F/116°C). Sprinkle a little cold water over the sides of a large bowl, pour in the mixture and cool for 15 minutes. Work the mixture in a figure-eight movement with a spatula until it becomes grainy, opaque and thick.

•

GREASE and line a 8 inch (20 cm) square cake pan with non-stick parchment (baking paper).

Whisk the eggs and sugar over a pan of gently simmering water until thick and creamy and the whisk leaves a heavy trail when lifted. Sift the flour, cornstarch and baking powder together twice and fold quickly and evenly through the mixture, then fold in the butter.

Turn into the prepared pan and cook in a moderately hot oven (375°F/190°C/Gas Mark 5) for about 25–30 minutes or until well risen and firm to the touch. Turn out onto a wire rack, peel off the paper and leave to cool.

Cut the cake into shapes — circles, ovals, squares or triangles. Brush each piece with apricot jam and leave for at least two hours. Shape the marzipan into small shapes and put one on top of each piece of cake.

Stand the bowl of fondant over a pan of gently simmering water and heat until just melted. If necessary dilute the fondant with a touch of cold water until it coats the back of a spoon. Divide the fondant into two or three bowls and shade each with a tiny amount of food dye. Place the cakes on wire racks and spoon the melted fondant over each piece of cake, letting the excess drip through the rack. Leave to dry. Drizzle glacé icing over the tops of the cakes.

Makes about 20 cakes

Frangipan Tarts

PATE SUCREE:

6 oz (175 g) all-purpose (plain) flour
pinch of salt
3 oz (90 g) superfine (caster) sugar
3 oz (90 g) butter, softened
3 egg yolks

1½ oz (40 g) ground almonds
good knob of butter, extra
Crème patissière
2 x 15 oz (450 g) cans apricot halves in
  juice
4 oz (125 g) apricot jam

TO MAKE the pastry, sift the flour and salt onto a flat surface, make a well in the middle and add the sugar, butter and egg yolks. Using the fingertips, pinch and work these ingredients together then gradually work in the flour to give a smooth pliable dough. Wrap in plastic (cling) wrap or foil and chill for an hour.

Roll out the pastry and use to line eight individual flan pans or Yorkshire pudding pans about 3½–4 inches (9–10 cm) in diameter. Bake blind in a moderately hot oven (375°F/190°C/Gas Mark 5) for 10–15 minutes, remove the paper and beans and return to the oven for a couple of minutes to dry out. Cool on a wire rack. Prepare the Crème patissière and fold in the almonds and extra butter while still hot.

Fill the pastry cases with the Crème patissière and arrange well-drained apricot halves (reserve the juice) on top to cover the filling.

Put the apricot jam into a saucepan with 4 tablespoons of the reserved apricot juice, dissolve and then boil until syrupy. Sieve and when cool spoon or brush over the apricots. Chill until required.

Makes 8

CREME PATISSIERE

•

1¼ cups (10 fl oz/300 ml)
milk

2 oz (60 g) superfine
(caster) sugar

¾ oz (20 g) all-purpose
(plain) flour

½ oz (15 g) cornstarch
(cornflour)

1 egg and 1 egg yolk
few drops of almond
extract (essence)

•

Heat the milk in a pan; blend the sugar, flours and eggs to a smooth paste, add a little milk and pour into the pan and cook very gently, stirring, until it boils and thickens. Simmer for a minute, remove from the heat and add the extract. Cover with plastic (cling) wrap and leave to cool.

•

French Apple Flans

1 recipe quantity Paté sucrée (page 51)
FILLING:
1 lb (900 g) cooking apples, peeled,
    cored and sliced
4 tablespoons water
10 oz (300 g) apricot jam, sieved

superfine (caster) sugar to taste
3 dessert apples
juice of ½ lemon
1 oz (30 g) butter, melted
1 tablespoon water

THESE FLANS are individual rich pastry cases with a layer of spiced apple purée topped with slices of apple glazed with butter and apricot glaze.

Place the apples and water in a saucepan and cook for about 20 minutes to make a smooth purée. Add a third of the apricot jam and the sugar to taste, and simmer very gently until the purée is very thick. Allow to cool.

Roll the pastry out thinly and use to line eight individual fluted flan pans of about 4–4½ inches (12–14 cm) in diameter.

Spoon the cold apple purée into the lined pans, levelling the top. Peel, core and thinly slice the dessert apples. Place them in a bowl with the lemon juice (to prevent browning); arrange in overlapping slices to cover the apple purée. Brush lightly with melted butter.

Cook in a moderately hot oven (400°F/200°C/Gas Mark 6) for about 35–40 minutes or until the apples are lightly browned and the pastry cooked through.

Place the remaining sieved apricot jam in a saucepan with the water and heat until the glaze thickens sufficiently to cover the back of a spoon.

Brush the warm glaze over the apple slices and the top edges of the pastry flans as soon as they come out of the oven. Leave to cool in the pans and then remove carefully to serve.

Makes 8

Fruit and Nut Cake

6 oz (175 g) prunes, finely chopped

4 oz (125 g) dried apricots, finely chopped

⅔ cup (5 fl oz/150 ml) dark rum

6 oz (175 g) butter or soft margarine

6 oz (175 g) dark soft brown or molasses sugar

3 eggs

8 oz (250 g) all-purpose (plain) flour

⅓ level teaspoon double-acting baking powder (¾ level teaspoon baking powder)

1 level teaspoon ground allspice

¼ level teaspoon ground ginger

4 oz (125 g) chopped mixed nuts (e.g. pecans, almonds, hazelnuts etc.)

6 oz (175 g) seedless raisins

grated peel (rind) of 1 lemon

grated peel (rind) of 1 orange

2 oz (60 g) mixed peel (rind), chopped

1 tablespoon dark treacle

Topping

TOPPING

•

about 4 tablespoons redcurrant jelly or apricot jam, melted and sieved

selection of shelled mixed nuts (e.g. brazils, pecans, almonds, walnuts)

a few prunes and/or dried apricots

halved glacé cherries

angelica, cut into strips

pieces of glacé pineapple

•

To make the topping for the fruit and nut cake, brush the cold cake with jelly or jam and arrange an attractive decoration of nuts, prunes, cherries, angelica and pineapple on the top. Brush again with more jelly or jam and leave to set.

•

PUT THE prunes and apricots into a bowl with 6 tablespoons of the rum and leave to stand for at least 15 minutes and preferably longer while preparing the rest.

Line the sides of a 10 inch (25 cm) spring form cake pan fitted with a tubular base with two strips of non-stick parchment (baking paper), and grease the base thoroughly.

Cream the butter and sugar together until very light and fluffy and pale. Beat in the eggs one at a time, following each with a spoonful of the flour. Sift the rest of the flour with the baking powder and spices and fold into the mixture.

Fold in the remaining ingredients, the prunes and apricots and their liquid. Turn into the prepared pan and carefully level the top.

Tie a treble thickness piece of newspaper around the outside of the pan and cook in a cool oven (300°F/150°C/Gas Mark 2), standing the pan on a folded sheet of newspaper in the oven, for about 1¾ hours or until a skewer inserted in the cake comes out clean. Leave in the pan until cold. Decorate with Topping before serving.

The cake may be stored in an airtight container for up to four weeks.

Fudge Brownies

4 oz (125 g) semi-sweet (plain) chocolate

5 oz (150 g) butter or margarine

12 oz (375 g) superfine (caster) or light soft brown sugar

½ teaspoon vanilla extract (essence)

4 eggs

5 oz (150 g) all-purpose (plain) flour, sifted

2 oz (60 g) walnuts or other nuts, finely chopped

3 oz (90 g) seedless raisins

little sifted cocoa powder

or ½ recipe quantity Chocolate fudge frosting (page 27)

or about 4 oz (125 g) semi-sweet (plain) or white chocolate, melted

> •
>
> Fudge Brownies can be frozen, undecorated, for up to three months
>
> •

LINE a rectangular pan 11 x 7 x 1½ inches (28 x 18 x 4 cm) with non-stick parchment (baking paper).

Break up the chocolate and place in an ovenproof bowl with the butter. Melt over a pan of gently simmering water, then beat in the sugar and extract until smooth. Beat in the eggs one at a time until smooth and quite evenly mixed.

Fold in the flour, followed by the nuts and raisins. Mix until evenly blended, then pour into the prepared pan.

Cook in a moderate oven (350°F/180°C/Gas Mark 4) for about 50 minutes or until well risen, firm to the touch and beginning to shrink away from the sides of the pan.

Leave to cool in the pan and then remove carefully and peel off the paper. Dredge generously with cocoa powder or make up the Chocolate fudge frosting and spread over the brownies, swirling attractively; or spread with the melted chocolate, again swirling it around. Leave to set.

Cut the brownies into fingers or squares to serve.

Makes 20–24

Gateau Japonais

3 egg whites
8 oz (250 g) superfine (caster) sugar
8 oz (250 g) ground almonds
few drops almond extract (essence)
½ recipe quantity Coffee crème au
   beurre (page 73)
3 oz (90 g) flaked almonds or chopped
   hazelnuts, toasted

Coffee glacé icing
1 oz (30 g) semi-sweet (plain) chocolate,
   melted
blanched almonds, lightly toasted or
   whole hazelnuts

LINE a jelly (Swiss) roll pan 13 x 9 inches (33 x 23 cm) with non-stick parchment (baking paper).

Whisk the egg whites until very stiff then fold in the sugar, almonds and almond extract. Spread this mixture evenly into the prepared pan.

Cook in a slow oven (300°F/150°C/Gas Mark 2) for about 1 hour until firm. Remove carefully to a wire rack and leave to cool; then peel off the paper and cut the cake crosswise into three even pieces.

Use some of the Coffee crème au beurre to sandwich the layers together and a little more to spread thinly around the side of the gateau. Carefully coat the sides in flaked almonds and stand on a serving dish.

Pour Coffee glacé icing over the top of the gateau and spread out with a palette knife dipped in hot water, but don't let it run down the sides. Decorate with almonds or hazelnuts. Put the melted chocolate into a paper icing bag, cut the tip off the icing bag and pipe thin lines across the gateau.

Serves 8

COFFEE GLACE ICING

•

6 oz (175 g)
confectioners' (icing)
sugar, sifted
2 teaspoons coffee extract
or very strong black coffee
little hot water

•

To make the glacé icing, put the sugar into a bowl and beat in the coffee extract and sufficient hot water to give a thick coating consistency.

•

Hazelnut Meringues

2 egg whites
5 oz (150 g) confectioners' (icing) sugar, sifted
1½ oz (40 g) hazelnuts, toasted and chopped

1 cup (8 fl oz/250 g) heavy (double) cream
1 tablespoon coffee extract (essence) or milk
9–10 cape gooseberries or kumquats
2–3 kiwi fruit, peeled

COVER two baking sheets with non-stick parchment (baking paper).

Put the egg whites and sugar into a heatproof bowl and place over a saucepan of gently simmering water. Whisk the mixture until it stands in stiff peaks; a hand-held electric mixer is best for this task.

Remove the bowl from the heat and continue to whisk for a minute or so and then beat in the chopped nuts. Spoon the mixture into a piping bag fitted with the largest plain vegetable nozzle and pipe into rounds of about 2½–3 inches (7–7½ cm) in diameter on the baking sheets.

Cook in a cool oven (300°F/150°C/Gas Mark 2) for about 30 minutes or until pale cream and easily removed from the paper. Cool on the paper. When cold they may be stored in an airtight container for up to two weeks before use.

To serve, whip the cream with the coffee extract or milk until stiff enough to pipe, but not over stiff. Put into a piping bag fitted with a large star vegetable nozzle and pipe a large whirl on top of each meringue. Decorate with cape gooseberries or kumquats and halved slices of peeled kiwi fruit. Chill until required.

Makes 9–10

•

Other nuts such as chopped pecans or walnuts or toasted chopped almonds may be used in place of the hazelnuts. Chocolate curls or caraque (page 77) may be used for decoration in place of fruit.

•

Lemon Drizzle Cake

6 oz (175 g) butter or margarine

6 oz (175 g) superfine (caster) sugar

3 eggs

6 oz (175 g) self-rising (raising) flour

grated peel (rind) of 2 small lemons

1 tablespoon lemon juice

TOPPING:

4 oz (125 g) superfine (caster) sugar

2 tablespoons lemon juice

FILLING:

3 oz (90 g) butter

6 oz (175 g) confectioners' (icing) sugar,
   sifted

2–3 teaspoons lemon juice

grated peel (rind) of 1 small lemon

about 6 tablespoons lemon curd

Grease and line the base of two 8 inch (20 cm) sandwich pans with non-stick parchment (baking paper); dust lightly with flour.

Cream the butter and sugar until very light and fluffy and pale. Beat in the eggs one at a time, following each with a tablespoon of flour. Sift the remaining flour and fold into the mixture with the lemon peel and juice. Divide between the pans, level the tops and cook in a moderately hot oven (375°F/190°C/Gas Mark 5) for about 20–25 minutes or until well risen, golden brown and firm to the touch. Cool briefly in the pans, then turn out onto a wire rack, peeling off the paper and keeping one cake with the top upwards.

Quickly mix the sugar and sufficient lemon juice together to give a thick but spreading consistency and pour over the cake with its top upwards, spreading out evenly; leave to set and cool.

For the filling, cream the butter then gradually beat in the sugar with enough lemon juice to give a thick spreading consistency; beat in the lemon peel.

Stand the plain cake on a serving plate and spread with most of the lemon curd then spread with half the butter cream. Carefully place the sugar coated cake on top, taking care not to crack the sugar glaze. Spread or pipe the remaining butter cream over the top and pipe a decorative pattern with the remaining lemon curd.

Lemon Praline Ring

4 oz (125 g) butter or margarine

5 oz (150 g) superfine (caster) sugar or
light soft brown sugar

3 eggs

3 oz (90 g) self-rising (raising) flour

3 oz (90 g) cornstarch (cornflour)

¼ level teaspoon double-acting baking
powder (½ level teaspoon baking
powder)

grated peel (rind) of 2 lemons

LEMON CREME AU BEURRE:

6 oz (175 g) butter, preferably unsalted

2 egg yolks

1 lb (500 g) confectioners' (icing) sugar,
sifted

1 tablespoon Grand Marnier, rum or
lemon juice

finely grated peel (rind) of 1 lemon
(optional)

Praline

TO MAKE the cake, grease a 1¾ pint (1 litre) ring pan and dust lightly with flour.

Cream the butter and sugar together until very light and fluffy and pale. Beat in the eggs one at a time following each with a tablespoon of flour. Sift the remaining flour, cornstarch and baking powder together and fold into the mixture with the lemon peel.

Turn into the prepared pan, level the top and cook in a moderate oven (350°F/180°C/Gas Mark 4) for about 45 minutes or until firm to the touch and just beginning to shrink from the sides of the pan. Loosen, turn out and cool on a wire rack.

To make the crème au beurre, melt the butter in a saucepan, remove from the heat and beat in the egg yolks. Gradually beat in the confectioners' sugar alternately with the liqueur, rum or lemon juice until light and fluffy. Beat in the lemon peel.

To assemble, cut the cake horizontally into three layers and sandwich back together with some of the crème au beurre. Use the crème au beurre to completely mask the cake and then cover evenly with the crushed Praline.

PRALINE

4 oz (125 g) superfine
(caster) sugar

1 tablespoon water

4 oz (125 g) unblanched
almonds

•

Put the sugar into a heavy-based saucepan with the water, heat gently, stirring until the sugar has dissolved. Bring to a boil, add the almonds and boil until it becomes a rich golden brown; shake frequently but do not stir. Pour onto an oiled surface or sheet of non-stick parchment (baking paper) and leave until cold. Crush the praline with the end of rolling pin or in a food processor or blender.

•

Linzertorte

6 oz (175 g) butter
3 oz (90 g) superfine (caster) sugar
finely grated peel (rind) of 1 lemon or
  orange
1 egg
8 oz (250 g) all-purpose (plain) flour
¼ level teaspoon double-acting baking
  powder (½ level teaspoon baking
  powder)

¾ level teaspoon ground cinnamon or
  mixed spice
2 oz (60 g) almonds, hazelnuts, walnuts,
  or pecan nuts, finely chopped
FILLING:
8 oz (250 g) raspberries, thawed if
  frozen
8 oz (250 g) raspberry jam

TO MAKE the pastry, cream the butter and sugar together until light and creamy then beat in the lemon or orange peel and the egg. Sift the flour with the baking powder and spice and work into the mixture followed by the chopped nuts. Wrap in plastic (cling) wrap or foil and chill until firm — about 45 minutes.

Lightly grease a 8–9 inch (20–23 cm) loose-based flan pan.

Combine the raspberries with the jam. Roll out about two-thirds of the pastry on a lightly floured surface with care for it is a rather dry consistency, and use to line the flan pan. Level the edges.

Spoon the raspberry mixture into the case and level the top. Roll out the remaining pastry and cut into narrow strips about ⅓ inch (1 cm) wide and use to make a lattice over the raspberry filling. Attach the ends to the side of the flan case.

Cook the flan in a moderately hot oven (375°F/190°C/Gas Mark 5) for 40–50 minutes or until firm and a light golden brown.

Mille-feuilles

12 oz (375 g) puff pastry

GLACE ICING:

6 oz (175 g) confectioners' (icing) sugar, sifted

1–2 tablespoons lemon juice or warm water

1 level tablespoon cocoa powder, sifted

FILLING:

⅔ cup (5 fl oz/150 ml) heavy (double) cream or ½ recipe quantity Crème patissière (page 51)

6–8 tablespoons raspberry or other jam

ROLL OUT the pastry thinly and trim to a 12 inch (30 cm) square. Cut the pastry in half and then cut each piece into strips measuring 6 x 2 inches (15 x 5 cm).

Place the pastry strips on dampened baking sheets, prick lightly and leave to rest for 10 minutes.

Cook in a very hot oven (450°F/230°C/Gas Mark 8) for about 10–15 minutes or until well puffed up and golden brown. Cool on wire racks. Select six pieces of pastry with the best tops.

To make the glacé icing, sift the sugar into a bowl and beat in sufficient lemon juice or warm water to give a thick coating consistency. Remove about 2 tablespoons of icing and beat in the sifted cocoa and put into a paper icing bag without a nozzle.

Quickly spread the white icing over the six best pieces of pastry and then make feathered icing using the cocoa icing. Leave to set.

To assemble, either whip the cream until stiff or make up the Crème patissière and leave to cool. If you want a chocolate filling, sift the cocoa powder into the milk before heating. Spread the remaining bases first with the jam and then with whipped cream or Crème patissière and position the iced layers on top, pressing gently to give an even shape.

Makes 6

FEATHERED ICING

•

Cut the tip off a paper icing bag and pipe lines down the length of each piece of pastry, keeping them equidistant. Immediately take a skewer and draw across these lines first in one direction and then the other, keeping about ¾ inch (2 cm) apart to give feathering effect.

•

Mocha Boxes

6 oz (175 g) butter or soft margarine

6 oz (175 g) superfine (caster) or light
soft brown sugar

3 eggs

6 oz (175 g) self-rising (raising) flour,
sifted

1 tablespoon coffee extract

CHOCOLATE RUM BUTTER CREAM:

6 oz (175 g) butter, preferably unsalted

10–12 oz (300–375 g) confectioners'
(icing) sugar, sifted

1½ oz (40 g) semi-sweet (plain)
chocolate, melted

1–2 tablespoons rum

8 oz (250 g) semi-sweet (plain) or
cake-covering chocolate, extra

GREASE and line the base of a 8 inch (20 cm) square cake pan with non-stick parchment (baking paper).

To make the cake, cream the butter and sugar together until light and fluffy then beat in the eggs, one at a time, adding a spoonful of flour after each one. Gradually fold in the remaining flour alternately with the coffee extract.

Put the cake mixture into the prepared pan, cook in a moderately hot oven (375°F/190°C/Gas Mark 5) for 50 minutes or until firm to the touch. Turn out of the pan onto a wire rack and leave until cold; cut into 2 inch (5 cm) squares.

For the butter cream, cream the butter until soft then gradually beat in the sugar alternately with the melted chocolate and the rum to give a spreading consistency.

Melt the extra chocolate and spread out thinly and evenly on a sheet of non-stick parchment (baking paper). When it begins to set mark into 80 pieces to fit the sides of the cake squares — just under 2 inches (5 cm) wide by the height of the cake. When dry, carefully peel off the paper. Scrape up the chocolate trimmings and repeat until you have enough squares.

Spread butter cream around the sides and over the top of each piece of cake then cover with five pieces of chocolate to form the box.

Makes 16

Mocha Cream Cake

6 oz (175 g) butter or soft margarine
6 oz (175 g) light soft brown sugar
3 eggs
5 oz (150 g) self-rising (raising) flour
1 oz (30 g) cocoa powder

¼ level teaspoon double-acting baking
    powder (½ level teaspoon baking
    powder)
1 tablespoon coffee extract (essence)
Coffee crème au beurre
confectioners' (icing) sugar, for dusting
chocolate coffee beans, for decoration

GREASE and line the base of two 8 inch (20 cm) round sandwich pans with non-stick parchment (baking paper) and dredge lightly with flour.

Cream the butter and sugar together until light and fluffy and pale. Beat in the eggs one at a time, following each with a spoonful of flour. Sift the rest of the flour with the cocoa powder and baking powder and fold into the mixture alternately with the coffee extract. Divide the mixture between the pans and level the tops. Cook in a moderately hot oven (375°F/190°C/Gas Mark 5) for 20–25 minutes or until well risen and just firm to the touch. Turn the cakes out carefully onto a wire rack and leave until cold.

To assemble the cake, place one cake on a serving plate and spread an even layer of crème au beurre over it. Then in the middle of the cake make a mound of about 3 inches (7½ cm) in diameter rising to a point in the middle. Put the rest of the crème au beurre into a piping bag fitted with a large star nozzle.

Cut the other cake into eight even wedges and dispose of one of them. Arrange the other seven on the cake so the points tip upwards in the middle. Dust the cake with confectioners' sugar.

Using the piping bag, pipe a shell or wavy line of crème au beurre between the slices beginning at the outer edge and finishing in the middle. Complete with a whirl in the middle of the cake. Decorate with chocolate coffee beans.

COFFEE CREME AU BEURRE:

•

8 oz (250 g) butter,
preferably unsalted
1 lb (500 g) confectioners'
(icing) sugar, sifted
1–2 tablespoons coffee
extract
1 egg yolk

•

Cream the butter until soft then gradually beat in the confectioners' sugar alternately with the coffee extract; add the egg yolk. If the mixture seems a little too stiff, add a touch of warm water to get the correct consistency for piping.

•

Orange and Lemon Kugelhupf

8 oz (250 g) butter or soft margarine
8 oz (250 g) superfine (caster) sugar
3 eggs
8 oz (250 g) self-rising (raising) flour, sifted
1 tablespoon orange or lemon juice
grated peel (rind) of 2 oranges and 1 lemon
2 oz (60 g) mixed peel, chopped
3 oz (90 g) golden raisins (sultanas)

SYRUP:
3 tablespoons orange juice
2 tablespoons lemon juice
3 oz (90 g) superfine (caster) sugar
DECORATION:
thinly pared peel (rind) of 1 small orange and 1 small lemon
5 tablespoons boiling water
2 oz (60 g) superfine (caster) sugar
Orange glacé icing

ORANGE GLACE ICING

•

4 oz (125 g) confectioners' (icing) sugar, sifted
about 2 teaspoons orange juice or orange flower water
few drops orange food dye
½ oz (15 g) butter, melted and cooled

•

Put the sugar into a bowl and gradually work in the orange juice or orange flower water and orange food dye followed by the melted butter to give a thick spreading consistency. If too soft, add a little more sifted sugar.

•

GREASE a 7½ cup (3 pint/1.7 litre) kugelhupf or ring pan with melted butter.

Cream the butter and sugar together until very light and fluffy. Beat in the eggs one at a time, following each with a spoonful of the flour. Fold in the remaining flour alternately with the fruit juice, then fold in the fruit peels, mixed peel and raisins. Turn into the pan and level the top. Stand on a baking sheet and cook in a moderately hot oven (375°F/190°C/Gas Mark 5) for about 1 hour or until well risen and firm to the touch. Test with a skewer to make sure it comes out clean. Turn out carefully onto a wire rack.

To make the syrup, blend the fruit juices and sugar together, bring to the boil for 2 minutes, then carefully spoon over the warm cake and leave until cold.

Wrap the cold cake in foil or put in an airtight container for 24 hours. Cut the fruit peel into julienne strips. Cook in a little boiling water for 5 minutes, add the sugar and continue for a further 5 minutes or until syrupy. Drain.

Stand the cake on a serving plate and pour the icing over the top, allowing it to run down the sides. Sprinkle with the orange and lemon peel.

Orange Caraque Gateau

6 oz (175 g) butter or soft margarine
6 oz (175 g) superfine (caster) sugar
3 eggs
6 oz (175 g) self-rising (raising) flour
3 tablespoons orange juice
grated peel (rind) of 1–2 oranges
6 tablespoons Grand Marnier

Orange crème au beurre mousseline
about 6 oz (175 g) orange curd
    or lemon curd with the grated peel
    (rind) of 1 orange added
6 oz (175 g) semi-sweet (plain)
    chocolate, for grating and caraque

GREASE and line the base of a rectangular pan 11 x 7 x 1½ inches (28 x 18 x 4 cm) with non-stick parchment (baking paper).

Cream the butter and sugar until light and fluffy and very pale. Beat in the eggs one at a time, following each with a spoonful of the flour. Fold in the remaining flour alternately with 1 tablespoon orange juice and the grated peel. Put into the prepared pan. Cook in a moderately hot oven (375°F/190°C/Gas Mark 5) for 25–30 minutes or until well risen and firm to the touch. Turn out onto a wire rack and leave until cold. Combine the remaining orange juice with the liqueur and sprinkle all over the cake. Leave to stand for about 1 hour.

Cut the cake in half lengthways to give two long slabs and sandwich together with a little of the crème au beurre and the orange or lemon curd. Use the rest of the crème au beurre to cover the cake.

Press 2 oz (60 g) grated chocolate over the top and sides of the gateau. For the caraque melt 4 oz (125 g) chocolate. Using a knife spread the melted chocolate thinly over a cool flat surface and leave until just set. Draw a sharp knife over the chocolate, scraping off long scrolls or curls. Arrange on the top of the gateau.

Serves 8

ORANGE CREME AU BEURRE MOUSSELINE

•

2½ oz (65 g) superfine (caster) sugar
4 tablespoons water
2 egg yolks
5 oz (150 g) butter, preferably unsalted
finely grated peel (rind) of 1 orange

•

Heat the sugar and water until the sugar dissolves, then boil until it forms a thread when tested between finger and thumb (225°F/107°C). Beat the egg yolks lightly. Gradually pour the syrup onto the egg yolks, beating until cool. Whisk in the butter a bit at a time then the peel.

•

Palmier Creams

8 oz (250 g) puff pastry, thawed if
    frozen
superfine (caster) sugar
FILLING:
8 fl oz (250 ml) heavy (double) cream
1½ level teaspoons confectioners'
    (icing) sugar, sifted

few drops vanilla or almond extract
    or 1 tablespoon rum or other liqueur
little jam (apricot, raspberry,
    strawberry, blackcurrant, gooseberry
    or quince)

> •
>
> *For spicy palmiers, mix 1 level teaspoon ground cinnamon or mixed spice with the sugar before dredging the pastry. Palmiers may also be served plain, if preferred.*
>
> •

LIGHTLY grease two or three baking sheets. Roll out the pastry thinly on a lightly floured surface and trim to a rectangle of about 12 x 10 inches (30 x 25 cm). Dredge with superfine sugar. Fold the long sides halfway to the middle of the pastry and dredge again with sugar. Fold the folded sides right to the middle of the pastry and dredge again with sugar; then fold in half lengthways to hide all the other folds. Press together lightly.

Cut through the fold into 12 even slices and place, cut sides downwards and well apart, on the baking sheets. Open the tip of each a little and flatten slightly with a round-bladed knife.

Dredge with a little more sugar and cook in a hot oven (425°F/220°C/Gas Mark 7) for 7–10 minutes until golden brown. Turn over carefully and continue to cook for a further 4–5 minutes until golden brown. Cool on a wire rack. At this stage the palmiers may be stored, when cold, in an airtight container.

To serve, whip the cream until stiff and fold in the sugar and extract or liqueur. Spread six of the palmiers with a thin layer of jam and then cover liberally with whipped cream. Top with a second palmier and serve or chill until required.

Makes 6 pairs

Paris Brest

1½ recipe quantities choux pastry
    (page 37)
1 recipe quantity Crème patissière
    (page 51)
1¼ cups (10 fl oz/300 ml) heavy
    (double) cream
2 tablespoons rum or any liqueur
    (optional)

8 oz (250 g) strawberries or raspberries
    or 6 oz (175 g) each green and black
    grapes, halved and depipped
1 oz (30 g) flaked almonds, toasted
confectioners' (icing) sugar, for
    dusting

MAKE UP the choux pastry and put into a piping bag fitted with a ¾ inch (2 cm) plain vegetable nozzle. Draw a 9 inch (23 cm) circle on a sheet of non-stick parchment (baking paper) and place on a baking sheet.

Pipe a ring of choux pastry to cover the drawn line, then pipe another one just inside the first one so it touches, then pipe a third ring over the join of the first two rings. If preferred the pastry may be spooned and spread into shape.

Cook in a hot oven (425°F/220°C/Gas Mark 7) for about 40–50 minutes until well risen and golden brown. If over browning, lay a sheet of waxed (greaseproof) paper over it. Cool on a wire rack.

Whip the cream until stiff, beat in the rum if used and then fold into the Crème patissière. Split the choux ring in half and scoop out any damp pastry. Stand the base on a serving dish and use half of the cream mixture to fill the ring.

Arrange the strawberries on top of the cream. Put the remaining cream over the fruit. Replace the lid, scatter the almonds over the top and then dredge with sifted confectioners' sugar.

Serves 8–10

Pithiviers Gateau

12 oz (350 g) puff pastry, thawed if
 frozen
FILLING:
3½ oz (90 g) blanched almonds
3½ oz (90 g) superfine (caster) sugar

1½ oz (40 g) butter
2 egg yolks
½ teaspoon vanilla extract (essence) or 1
 tablespoon orange flower water or rum
beaten egg to glaze

ROLL OUT the pastry on a floured surface and cut into two rounds of 9 inches
(23 cm), leaving one just a little thinner than the other.

Place the thinner pastry round on a dampened baking sheet.

To make the filling, grind the almonds in a food processor or grinder to a
paste; add the sugar and butter gradually then work in the egg yolks followed by
the extract or orange flower water or rum until the paste becomes soft and creamy
and pale.

Spread the almond filling in the middle of the pastry leaving a 1½ inch (4 cm)
border all round and making sure it is spread evenly.

Damp the edges of the pastry round with water, position the pastry lid and
press the edges firmly together.

Flake the edges and crimp if liked, then glaze with the beaten egg. Using a
sharp knife mark a "cartwheel" pattern on top of the pastry.

Cook in a hot oven (425°F/220°C/Gas Mark 7) for 25–30 minutes until well
risen and golden brown. Leave until cold.

Serve the gateau cut into wedges.

Serves 8

Polish Cheesecake Slices

1 recipe quantity Paté sucrée (page 51)

FILLING:

8 oz (250 g) full fat soft cream cheese

4 egg yolks

2 oz (60 g) butter, melted

8 oz (250 g) caster or light soft brown
   sugar

grated peel (rind) of 1 orange or lemon

1 tablespoon orange flower water

TOPPING:

6 oz (175 g) confectioners' (icing)
   sugar, sifted

few pieces glacé pineapple, glacé cherries
   and other glacé fruits

few pieces angelica, cut into narrow
   strips

ROLL OUT the pastry carefully and use to line a lightly greased rectangular pan
11 x 7 x 1½ inches (28 x 18 x 4 cm) and trim and crimp the edges.

To make the filling, beat the cheese until smooth and then beat in the egg
yolks, butter, sugar, fruit peel and orange flower water. Put into the pastry case
and level the top.

Cook in a moderate oven (350°F/180°C/Gas Mark 4) for about 1 hour or
until quite firm. Leave in the pan to cool. When cold cut into squares to serve.
Decorate each square with pieces of glacé fruit and angelica and sprinkle with
confectioners' sugar.

Makes 12

Sachertorte

5 oz (150 g) semi-sweet (plain)
  chocolate
5 oz (150 g) superfine (caster) sugar
4 oz (125 g) butter
4 eggs, separated
few drops vanilla extract (essence)
3 oz (90 g) all-purpose (plain) flour

¼ level teaspoon double-acting baking
  powder (½ level teaspoon baking
  powder)
10 oz (300 g) apricot jam or apricot
  preserve
Chocolate icing
gold drooges, to decorate

GREASE and line the base of a 8½ inch (22 cm) spring form cake pan with non-stick parchment (baking paper) and lightly dust with flour.

Melt the chocolate in a heatproof bowl over a pan of gently simmering water. Cream the sugar and butter together until very light and fluffy and pale. Beat in the egg yolks one at a time, followed by the melted chocolate and extract.

Sift the flour and baking powder together. Whisk the egg whites until stiff and dry and fold half into the cake mixture followed by half the flour, then fold in the remaining egg whites and flour.

Pour into the cake pan, level the top and cook in a very moderate oven (325°F/170°C/Gas Mark 3) for 1–1¼ hours until well risen, firm to the touch and a skewer inserted in the cake comes out clean. Turn out onto a wire rack.

When cold, split the cake in half horizontally and fill with half the jam. Reassemble the cake and stand on a serving plate or cake board and spread all over with the remaining jam.

Place 4 tablespoons of icing in a piping bag with a star nozzle. Carefully pour remaining icing over the cake and spread to cover the sides and top evenly. Pipe decorative swirls on top of the cake and decorate with gold drooges. Leave to set.

CHOCOLATE ICING

•

6 oz (175 g) semi-sweet
(plain) chocolate

1 cup (6 fl oz/175 ml)
water

1 heaped tablespoon
butter

4 oz (125 g) superfine
(caster) sugar

•

Melt the chocolate with 2 tablespoons of the water in a heatproof bowl over a pan of gently simmering water. Stir in the butter until melted. Boil the rest of the water with the sugar until at the thread stage (221°F/104°C). Pour over the chocolate and beat until smooth. Cool, beating from time to time until thick.

•

Savarin

8 oz (250 g) all-purpose (plain) white
    flour
pinch of salt
1 level tablespoon dried yeast
1 level teaspoon sugar
6 tablespoons warm milk
4 eggs, beaten
4 oz (125 g) butter, very soft

Syrup
FILLING:
1¼ cups (10 fl oz/300 ml) heavy
    (double) cream
3 tablespoons kirsch or brandy
8–12 oz (225–350 g) fresh fruit,
    prepared (e.g. strawberries,
    raspberries, melon balls, grapes, kiwi
    fruit, pineapple etc)
confectioners' (icing) sugar, for dusting

SIFT THE flour and salt into a bowl. Blend the dried yeast and sugar with half the milk and leave in a warm place for about 10 minutes until frothy and then add to the flour.

Add the rest of the milk and the eggs to the flour and work the mixture to a smooth dough, it should be very soft and almost runny. Beat vigorously until smooth and elastic. Cover the bowl with oiled plastic (cling) wrap and leave in a warm place until doubled in size — about 45 minutes.

Beat the butter into the dough until blended and turn into a well-buttered and floured ring pan 8 inches (20 cm) in diameter. Cover with oiled plastic (cling) wrap and put in a warm place until the dough has risen to the top of the pan.

Cook in a moderately hot oven (375°F/190°C/Gas Mark 5) for 30–40 minutes until golden brown and firm to the touch. Turn the pan onto a wire rack and leave upside down until the cake drops out.

Put a plate under the savarin (while still on the wire rack) and prick all over with a fork. Pour the syrup all over the savarin, spooning it over until it is all absorbed.

Remove the cold savarin carefully to a serving dish. Whip the cream with the kirsch until thick and use to fill the middle of the savarin alternately with the fruit.

SYRUP

•

6 oz (175 g) white sugar
1 cup (8 fl oz/250 ml)
water
strips of lemon peel (rind)
6 tablespoons kirsch or
brandy

•

Heat the sugar, water and lemon peel until dissolved then boil for 5 minutes. Remove from the heat, and stir in the kirsch.

•

Silver Sandwich Cake

3 egg whites
pinch of salt
12 oz (350 g) superfine (caster) sugar
4 oz (125 g) blended white fat
8 oz (250 g) self-rising (raising) flour
1 oz (30 g) cornstarch (cornflour)
¾ cup (6 fl oz/175 ml) milk
1 teaspoon vanilla extract (essence)

½ teaspoon almond extract (essence)
4 oz (125 g) apricot jam
2 oz (60 g) hazelnuts, toasted and finely
   chopped
2 recipe quantities Chocolate butter
   cream (page 25)
10–15 Frosted rose petals

Grease two 8 inch (20 cm) round sandwich pans and line bases with non-stick parchment (baking paper).

Whisk the egg whites and salt until very stiff and dry. Gradually whisk in 6 oz (175 g) of the sugar until the mixture forms stiff peaks again.

Cream the fat and remaining sugar together until light and fluffy. Sift the flour and cornstarch together and gradually beat into the creamed mixture alternately with the milk and extracts. Carefully fold in the whisked egg whites. Divide between the cake pans and level the tops. Cook in a moderately hot oven (375°F/190°C/Gas Mark 5) for about 30–35 minutes or until well risen and firm to the touch. Cool for a couple of minutes in the pans before turning out carefully onto wire racks. Leave until cold.

Spread one cake with apricot jam and then with a thin layer of Chocolate butter cream. Sandwich cakes together. Spread cake sides with apricot jam, lay the nuts on a sheet of waxed (greaseproof) paper and roll the cake in them so sides are covered. Stand the cake on a plate. Spread top with butter cream. When set arrange the frosted rose petals on the cake.

FROSTED ROSE PETALS

•

rose petals
egg whites
superfine (caster) sugar

•

Wash and dry the rose petals carefully. Lightly whisk the egg whites and paint each petal with it. Then dip immediately into sugar to coat thoroughly. Shake off the surplus and place on non-stick parchment (baking paper) to dry; leave in a warm place until quite dry and crisp. Frosted petals can be stored in an airtight container for a few days before use.

•

Spiced Apple and Cranberry Lattice

9 oz (250 g) self-rising (raising) flour
pinch of salt
2 level tablespoons custard powder or
cornstarch (cornflour)
¾ level teaspoon ground cinnamon,
allspice or mixed spice
3 oz (90 g) butter or margarine
grated peel (rind) of 1 orange (or lemon)
2½ oz (65 g) superfine (caster) sugar
1 egg yolk

6 tablespoons milk
FILLING:
1¼ lb (550 g) cooking apples, peeled,
cored and sliced
4–6 oz (100–175 g) cranberries
2 tablespoons water
2 level tablespoons clear honey
2 oz (60 g) light soft brown or superfine
(caster) sugar
whipped cream for decoration

SIFT THE flour with the salt, custard powder or cornstarch and spice into a bowl. Rub in the butter then mix the orange peel evenly through it followed by the sugar.

Add the egg yolk and sufficient milk to mix to a pliable dough and knead lightly until smooth, then wrap in foil and chill while making the filling.

Place the apples in a saucepan with the cranberries and water and cook very gently until just tender. Remove from the heat, stir in the honey and sugar until melted and then leave until cold.

Roll out two-thirds of the pastry dough and use to line a greased 11 x 7 inch (28 x 18 cm) rectangular pan. Cover with the apple and cranberry filling. Roll out the remaining pastry and cut into strips about ⅓ inch (1 cm) wide. Use to make a lattice over the apple filling, attaching the ends to the pastry with a dab of water.

Cook in a very hot oven (425°F/220°C/Gas Mark 7) for 10 minutes, then reduce the temperature to moderately hot (375°F/190°C/Gas Mark 5) and continue for about 20 minutes or until the pastry is golden brown and cooked through.

Makes 14–16 slices

Spiced Apple and Ginger Strudels

16 sheets filo pastry, thawed if frozen
2 oz (60 g) butter, melted
FILLING:
2 lb (900 g) cooking apples, peeled,
  cored and sliced
½ level teaspoon ground cinnamon or
  mixed spice
2 tablespoons ginger syrup from the
  preserved ginger

2 tablespoons water
4 oz (125 g) sugar or to taste
4–6 pieces preserved ginger, finely
  chopped
grated peel (rind) of 1 small orange
3 oz (90 g) ground almonds
confectioners' (icing) sugar, for dredging

•

VARIATIONS
To the apple add either
8 oz (250 g) cranberries;
4 oz (125 g) each
chopped dates and
chopped dried apricots;
or 8 oz (250 g)
blackcurrants or
blackberries or anything
else you fancy.

•

PLACE the apples in a saucepan with the cinnamon or mixed spice, ginger syrup and water. Bring to a boil, cover and simmer until tender — about 10 minutes. Remove from the heat and beat in the sugar to taste, ginger and orange peel. Cool.

Lay out four sheets of filo pastry, brush lightly with melted butter, cover each with another sheet then brush them with butter. Sprinkle half the ground almonds over the sheets.

Use half the apple filling to spread over the sheets, leaving a margin of about 1 inch (2½ cm) on one short side and both long sides and leaving about a third of the rest of it clear. Fold the narrow edges over the filling and, beginning at the narrow end with the filling, roll up loosely towards the wide border, keeping it neat and even. Stand the parcels on greased parchment (baking paper). Repeat with a further four sheets of filo.

Brush the eight strudels liberally with melted butter and cook in a moderately hot oven (375°F/190°C/Gas Mark 5) for 25 minutes or until golden brown and crisp. Cool on a wire rack. Serve dredged with confectioners' sugar.

Makes 8

Spiced Meringue Gateau

5 egg whites
10 oz (300 g) superfine (caster) sugar
1 level teaspoon ground cinnamon or
    mixed spice
1 recipe quantity Crème patissèrie
    (page 51)

FILLING
1¼ cups (10 fl oz/300 ml) heavy
    (double or whipping) cream
4 kiwi fruit
12 raspberries

DRAW a rectangle 11 x 4 inches (28 x 10 cm) on three sheets of non-stick parchment (baking paper) and place each on a baking sheet. Whisk the egg whites until very stiff and dry, gradually whisk in the sugar and spice, a spoonful at a time, making sure the meringue is stiff again before adding further sugar.

Put the meringue into a piping bag fitted with a large star vegetable nozzle and pipe zigzag lines to cover the rectangles. Also pipe six large meringue stars on the paper around the rectangles.

Cook in a very cool oven (225°F/110°C/Gas Mark ¼) for 2½–3 hours, moving the trays around in the oven after each hour, until crisp and dry and they peel off the paper easily. The stars will be ready after about 2 hours.

When cool, peel off the paper and store in an airtight container until required.

Whip the cream until thick but not too stiff and fold about three-quarters of it into the Crème patissière. Peel and slice the kiwi fruit and reserve six slices for decoration. Use the cream mixture to sandwich the three layers of meringue together along with the sliced kiwi fruit. Place on a serving dish.

Use the remaining cream to attach the meringue stars to the top of the gateau. Decorate between them with the remaining kiwi fruit and raspberries. Chill until ready to serve.

Serves 6–8

> The meringue rectangles and stars can be made up to a week in advance, but store with sheets of non-stick parchment (baking paper) between the layers. Other fruits in season may be used to fill and decorate the meringue.

Stollen

½ oz (15 g) dried yeast
2 tablespoons warm water
3 oz (90 g) light soft brown sugar
6 tablespoons warm milk
2 tablespoons rum
¼ level teaspoon almond extract (essence)
14 oz (400 g) all-purpose (plain) flour
pinch of salt
1 egg, beaten
5 oz (150 g) unsalted butter, softened

2 oz (60 g) seedless raisins
2 oz (60 g) glacé cherries, chopped
2 oz (60 g) golden raisins (sultanas)
1 oz (30 g) angelica, chopped
2 oz (60 g) mixed peel, chopped
1½ oz (40 g) flaked almonds
1½ oz (40 g) crystallized or glacé
    pineapple or papaya
4 oz (125 g) yellow marzipan
confectioners' (icing) sugar, for dredging

> •
> *This recipe is suitable to freeze for up to two months; to use thaw slowly and dredge with sugar.*
> •

BLEND the yeast in the water, add 1 teaspoon of the sugar and leave in a warm place until frothy. Dissolve 2 oz (60 g) of the sugar in the milk. Add the rum, extract and yeast liquid.

Sift the flour and salt into a bowl and make a well in the middle. Add the yeast mixture, egg, 3 oz (90 g) of the butter cut into small pieces and the fruits, nuts and pineapple or papaya. Mix to a soft dough and knead for 10 minutes on a lightly floured surface. Place the dough in an oiled plastic bag and put to rise in a warm place for about 2 hours or until doubled in size.

Knock back the dough and knead lightly until smooth then roll out to a rectangle 12 x 8 inches (30 x 20 cm). Brush with melted butter and sprinkle with the remaining sugar. Roll the marzipan into a sausage shape the length of the dough and place it down the middle. Wrap it in the dough and slightly taper the ends. Place on a greased baking sheet, brush with melted butter and leave in a warm place until almost doubled in size.

Cook in a moderately hot oven (375°F/190°C/Gas Mark 5) for about 45 minutes until well risen and browned. Cool on a wire rack. Before serving dredge with sifted confectioners' sugar.

Strawberry Shortcakes

8 oz (250 g) self-rising (raising) flour
½ level teaspoon double-acting baking
    powder (1 level teaspoon baking
    powder)
pinch of salt
3 oz (90 g) butter
2 oz (60 g) superfine (caster) sugar
1 egg, beaten
1–3 tablespoons milk

FILLING:
¾–1 lb (350–450 g) fresh strawberries
3 level tablespoons superfine (caster)
    sugar
1¼ cups (10 fl oz/300 ml) heavy
    (double) cream
few drops of vanilla extract (essence) or
    1 tablespoon rum

To make the shortcakes, sift the flour, baking powder and salt into a bowl and rub in the butter until the mixture resembles fine breadcrumbs. Stir in the sugar. Add the egg and sufficient milk to mix to a pliable dough. Knead lightly and divide the dough into eight even-sized pieces.

Roll out each piece of dough to a round of 3 inches (7½ cm) in diameter, or alternately stamp out into plain or fluted rounds using a cutter.

On a lightly greased baking sheet, cook in a moderately hot oven (375°F/ 190°C/Gas Mark 5) for about 15 minutes or until well risen and light golden brown. Cool on a wire rack.

To make the filling, reserve 8 large strawberries for decoration and slice the remainder into a bowl. Mix in the sugar. Whip the cream with the extract or rum and fold about half of it through the strawberries.

Split the shortcakes in half horizontally and use the strawberry cream mixture to fill them. Put the remaining whipped cream into a piping bag fitted with a large star vegetable nozzle and pipe a large whirl of cream on each shortcake. Top each with strawberries. Chill until ready to serve.

Makes 8

Strawberry Syllabub Tarts

PATE SUCREE:
4 oz (125 g) all-purpose (plain) flour
pinch of salt
2 oz (60 g) superfine (caster) sugar
2 oz (60 g) butter, softened
2 egg yolks

few drops vanilla extract
Syllabub filling
about 6 oz (175 g) strawberries
3 tablespoons redcurrant jelly
1 tablespoon water

SYLLABUB FILLING
•
1 egg white
2 oz (60 g) superfine (caster) sugar
finely grated peel (rind) of ½ lemon
a good pinch of finely grated orange peel (rind)
2 teaspoons lemon juice
4 tablespoons dry white wine
⅔ cup (5 fl oz/150 ml) heavy (double) cream
•
Whisk the egg white until very stiff then fold in the sugar followed by the fruit peels, lemon juice and wine. Whip the cream until stiff and fold through the syllabub mixture.
•

TO MAKE the pastry cases, sift the flour and salt into a pile on a flat surface and make a well in the middle. Add the sugar, butter, egg yolks and extract.

Work the sugar mixture together then gradually work in the flour to give a smooth pliable dough. Wrap in foil and chill for 20–30 minutes.

Roll out the pastry and use to line four individual flan pans 4–4½ inches (10–11 cm) in diameter or six deep fluted pans 3 inches (7½ cm) in diameter. Prick the bases and bake blind in a moderately hot oven (375°F/190°C/Gas Mark 5) for about 15 minutes; remove, then return to the oven for about 5 minutes to dry out and turn a light golden brown. Cool.

Fill the pastry cases with the Syllabub an hour before serving. If the strawberries are small they may be used whole or halved to place on top of the syllabub, if not, slice them and arrange attractively over the filling. Melt the redcurrant jelly with the water and boil for approximately 1 minute. Cool slightly, then carefully spoon or brush over the strawberries. Chill until ready to serve.

Makes 4–6

Strawberry Walnut Cake

4 eggs
4 oz (125 g) superfine (caster) sugar
4 oz (125 g) all-purpose (plain) flour
½ level teaspoon double-acting baking
    powder (1 level teaspoon baking
    powder)
4 oz (125 g) walnuts, finely chopped
1 oz (30 g) butter, melted and cooled
BUTTER CREAM:
3 oz (90 g) unsalted butter

6 oz (175 g) confectioners' (icing) sugar,
    sifted
1–2 tablespoons any orange liqueur
8 oz (250 g) whole strawberry jam
DECORATION:
1¼ cups (10 fl oz/300 ml) heavy
    (double) cream
8–12 small fresh strawberries
sprigs of fresh mint

Grease and line the bases of three 8 inch (20 cm) sandwich pans with non-stick parchment (baking paper).

Put the eggs and sugar into a large heatproof bowl over a pan of simmering water and whisk with an electric mixer for 8–10 minutes or until very pale and thick and the whisk leaves a heavy trail when lifted. Remove from the heat.

Sift the flour and baking powder together twice, then stir in the walnuts. Carefully fold this into the whisked mixture, then fold in the butter. Divide between the pans and cook in a moderate oven (350°F/180°C/Gas Mark 4) for 20–25 minutes until firm to the touch. Turn out and cool on wire racks.

To make the butter cream, cream the butter, then beat in the sugar alternately with the liqueur. Spread this over two of the cakes, followed by a thick layer of strawberry jam. Layer up the cakes leaving the top plain. Leave for 2–3 hours.

Whip the cream until stiff and use about half to cover the top of the cake. Put the remaining cream into a piping bag fitted with a large star nozzle and pipe whirls or scrolls on top. Decorate with whole strawberries and sprigs of mint.

Walnut and Raspberry Roll

4 eggs
3 oz (90 g) superfine (caster) sugar
1½ oz (40 g) all-purpose (plain) flour
¼ level teaspoon ground cinnamon or
    mixed spice
1½ oz (40 g) walnuts, ground

1 oz (30 g) butter, melted and cooled
4 oz (125 g) seedless raspberry jam
6–8 oz (175–225 g) raspberries
DECORATION:
confectioners' (icing) sugar, for dredging
8 large walnut halves

FILLING
•
1¼ cups (10 fl oz/300 ml)
heavy (double) cream
1 tablespoon rum or
brandy (optional)
good pinch of ground
cinnamon or mixed spice

•

Whip the cream until
stiff with the rum or
brandy added, if used,
and the spice.

GREASE and line a 12 x 10 inch (30 x 25 cm) jelly (Swiss) roll pan with non-stick parchment (baking paper) and dust lightly with flour.

Whisk the eggs and sugar in a large heatproof bowl over a saucepan of hot water until the mixture is thick and very pale and the whisk leaves a thick heavy trail when lifted. Remove from the heat and whisk for a couple of minutes longer.

Sift the flour and spice together twice and mix in the walnuts. Fold carefully into the whisked mixture using a metal spoon. Finally fold in the butter. Spread into the prepared pan, making sure there is ample in the corners. Cook in a moderately hot oven (375°F/190°C/Gas Mark 5) for 15–20 minutes or until just firm and springy.

Turn out onto a sheet of waxed (greaseproof) paper sprinkled with sugar. Peel off the lining paper and trim the edges. While warm, roll up with the paper inside. Cool on a wire rack.

Unroll the cake, remove paper and spread with jam, then with two-thirds of the filling. Reserve 6–8 raspberries and sprinkle the remainder over the filling.

Carefully reroll the cake, stand on a serving plate and dredge lightly with sugar. Put the remaining filling in a piping bag fitted with a large star vegetable nozzle and pipe a line of stars or shells along the top of the cake. Use the walnut halves and reserved raspberries for decoration.

Whiskey Layer Cake

7 oz (200 g) golden raisins (sultanas)
good ½ cup (5 fl oz /125 ml) water
4 oz (125 g) butter or margarine
5 oz (125 g) light soft brown sugar
1 egg
6 oz (175 g) all-purpose (plain) flour
l level teaspoon baking soda
(bicarbonate of soda)
½ level teaspoon ground cloves

¼ level teaspoon grated nutmeg
½ level teaspoon ground cinnamon
3 oz (90 g) walnuts, finely chopped
2 tablespoons whiskey
Whiskey butter cream
TOPPING:
6 oz (100 g) semi-sweet (plain) chocolate
1 heaped tablespoon of butter

WHISKEY BUTTER CREAM

•

3 oz (90 g) butter,
preferably unsalted
1 egg yolk
8 oz (250 g)
confectioners' (icing)
sugar, sifted
1 tablespoon whiskey

•

Melt the butter in a
saucepan, remove from
the heat and beat in the
egg yolk. Gradually beat
in the confectioners'
sugar, alternating with
the whiskey until light
and fluffy.

•

TO MAKE the cake, grease and base line two 8 inch (20 cm) deep sandwich or cake pans with greased waxed (greaseproof) or non-stick parchment (baking paper). Put the raisins and water into a small pan, bring to a boil and simmer gently for 15 minutes. Strain off the liquid and make up to ½ cup (4 fl oz/ 100 ml) with water. Leave to cool.

Cream the butter and sugar together until very pale and fluffy, then beat in the egg. Sift the flour with the soda and spices and fold into the mixture alternating with the raisin liquid. Add the walnuts, raisins and whiskey and mix lightly but evenly. Divide between the pans and level the tops.

Cook in a moderate oven (350°F/180°C/Gas Mark 4) for 30–35 minutes until firm. Cool briefly in the pan, then carefully loosen the edges and turn out very carefully onto wire racks to cool.

Use just over half the butter cream to sandwich the cakes together.

Melt the 4 oz (125 g) chocolate over a pan of gently simmering water, stir the butter into the chocolate and spread over the top of the cake; leave to set. Put the remaining butter cream into a piping bag fitted with a large star nozzle and pipe 9 whirls on top of the cake. Top with remaining 2 oz (60 g) chocolate grated.

Index